Staffordshire
Figures
of the
19th & 20th Centuries

A Collector's Guide

Staffordshire Figures

of the

19th & 20th Centuries

A Collector's Guide

Kit Harding

Special Consultants:
Adrian Harding
Nicholas Harding

MILLER'S STAFFORDSHIRE FIGURES OF THE
19TH & 20TH CENTURIES: A COLLECTOR'S GUIDE
by Kit Harding
Special Consultants: Adrian Harding and Nicholas Harding

First published in Great Britain in 2000 by Miller's, a division of
Mitchell Beazley, imprints of Octopus Publishing Group Ltd,
2–4 Heron Quays, London E14 4JP

Miller's is a registered trademark of Octopus Publishing Group Ltd

Copyright © Octopus Publishing Group Ltd 2000

Commissioning Editor **Anna Sanderson**
Executive Art Editor **Vivienne Brar**
Project Editor **Emily Anderson**
Editor **Mary Scott**
Designer **Louise Griffiths**
Indexer **Sue Farr**
Picture Research **Lois Charlton**
Production **Jessame Emms**
Jacket photograph **Steve Tanner**

ISBN 1 84000 307 3
A CIP catalogue record for this book is available from the British Library
Set in Bembo, Frutiger and Shannon
Produced by Toppan Printing Co., (HK) Ltd.
Printed and bound in China

contents

Introduction

Staffordshire figures were originally made as ornaments, to enliven a mantelpiece and to brighten up the home. Some had secondary uses such as spill vases, pastille-burners, watch holders and candlesticks, but their main purpose was decorative. Today the figures have become very popular collectors' pieces, and they have an international appeal beyond Britain.

This book includes figures from about 1835 until 1962, representing the most prolific period of manufacture of Staffordshire figures. Which Staffordshire pottery began the production of these figures is not known, nor which figures they began with. The majority of pieces were produced in the Victorian era, however, with the 1850s to 1870s witnessing their heyday in terms of quality of production. The Victorian figures, therefore, form the main focus of this book, though there are many figures after this period which merit attention and are also touched on.

Shortly after Queen Victoria ascended the throne in 1837, a major change occurred in the manufacture of Staffordshire figures. Up until then, these figures had been made mainly by hand, using many "secondary" moulds over and above the three basic moulds (front, back and base) which were required to make a standard figure, and were decorated all around. This was a time-consuming process and the figures were therefore expensive to produce. In the mid-1840s, however, a new design called the "flatback" was developed. The man who developed this revolutionary design, and for which pottery it was produced, is unknown. All that it required was a three-part mould, comprising a front, a back and a base. Clay was pressed by hand into the front and back moulds; the two moulds were then tied together and fired with the base attached. After firing, the figure, in a "biscuit" state (i.e. without a glaze), would then be decorated and fired again in the glazing kiln or "glost oven".

What was so innovative was not only that the number of moulds had been reduced to three, but the concept that, as the figure was

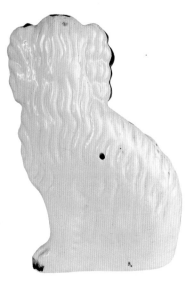

to stand on the mantelpiece or against a wall, there was no need to decorate the back as it would not be seen.

Very soon after the flatback design was conceived, "production lines" were introduced at most Staffordshire potteries. Parts of the process were allocated to different people, so that this new type of figure could be made at a low cost in quantities never before seen.

Over the next 40 years well over 5,000 different models of figures were made, some of them in great quantity, such as the comforter illustrated left. Figures of famous contemporary and historical personalities were popular: over 110 different portraits were potted, including more than 60 versions of Queen Victoria, 50 of Prince Albert, 20 of Garibaldi and 17 of Nelson. Religious, musical and theatrical figures were also produced, as were figures of children, soldiers, sailors, shepherds and hunters, animals and domestic buildings – from cottages to castles. Some versions were made in three or four sizes and some, such as the dog figures, in up to six.

Virtually all Victorian Staffordshire figures are unmarked, so it is not possible to identify the maker. On occasion, markings are found on the bottom of figures, but these are usually decorator's marks – made to indicate which colour should be applied, or whether underglaze blue was to be used, for example – and are of no real significance in terms of dating or identification. On the very rare occasions that a figure has been found with a maker's mark, it has been quite a late piece, after 1875.

A figure is therefore always judged on its quality and not on its maker. Flatbacks were made by pressing clay into the mould: each time this was done the mould deteriorated, thus no two figures are ever identical. The first figure made from the mould is the sharpest and the best, and usually these are also the better decorated. The keen collector will recognize this and pay for the finer figures accordingly.

With such a range to choose from, most collectors concentrate on specific areas of interest, and the more collectors there are for a particular subject area, the higher the prices will be: if you choose to collect wild animals or political figures, for example, you will need to dig deep. However there are still many bargains to be found if you know what to look for, even within popular fields.

Many of the figures have a story to tell, be it that of a murderer and his mistress, a morganatic marriage, a failed politician, a daring rescue, a battle won, a damsel in distress, a soldier's fare-well, a sailor's return, or just a melodramatic moment. Many figures are still unidentified and awaiting the discovery of a print, playbill or source which will identify them – one of the greatest joys of collecting Staffordshire figures. These figures not only portray personalities, they offer a glimpse of scenes and occupations long gone.

Prices & dimensions

Prices vary depending on the condition of the figure, the rarity and where it is purchased, so the prices given are an approximate guide only. The sterling/dollar conversion has been made at a rate of £1 = $1.60 (adjust the dollar value as necessary to accord with current exchange rates). Height is given to the nearest half centimetre/quarter inch and refers to the figure illustrated.

Collecting advice

Victorian Staffordshire figures started to be collected seriously in the late 1950s and early 1960s. Many of the first collectors were Americans, who bought mostly animals, including dogs, and decorative figures (generally pastoral scenes); in England portraits of famous contemporary and historical figures were collected. Up until the mid-1970s prices were still fairly low, and a pair of dogs, for example, could still be purchased for £15/$25. Since that time, however, the situation has changed, and now all figures are avidly sought after. There are a number of specialist dealers, and many auction houses hold sales devoted to the subject, but bargains can still be found.

What to collect

The range of Staffordshire figures produced was enormous, and usually the collector decides on a particular subject or category which is of interest, and collects as many figures in that subject as his or her inclination or purse allows. There are a number of established fields, such as Portrait, Royalty, Theatre, Politicians, Military, Murderers, the Crimean War, Sport, Animals and Dogs. If the new or novice collector chooses any of these they will find considerable competition and consequently high prices. There are also crossovers between categories, resulting in even more competition, for instance the Duke of Cambridge can be collected by a Military, Royalty, Portrait or Crimean War collector, so it is advisable to pursue a single interest.

Dating can be a problem: the last "Victorian" Staffordshire figures were made in 1962 when the Kent factory ceased production, and it is difficult to determine whether many of these Kent figures were made in 1910 or 1960, as the only detectable differences are in the decoration. Figures were produced from these moulds as early as 1850 and it is the earlier pieces that are most sought after. Later figures are still comparatively inexpensive, though this situation may not last.

The figures illustrated in this book span the entire period. No two figures are identical, and if the figure is in superb condition, sharply modelled and delicately decorated, it will fetch a much higher price than one which is late from the mould or "in the white" (uncoloured).

Care and cleaning

Take care with cleaning: if the figure is dirty, stand it in a plastic bowl and wash it with soapy water, using a sponge or soft tooth-brush for the crevices. Most figures that are not spill vases have a small hole in them either at the back (see figure on p.6) or the base, to allow hot air inside to escape in the kiln. If the figure is soaked the hole will fill with water, so ensure that it drains to avoid later leakage. The figures are glazed with a thin layer of glass, so a proprietary glass cleaner will remove dust. Do not attempt to repair or restore your figure – this must be left to a professional. Any repairs you carry out will only depreciate the value and increase any subsequent cost.

Repairs and restoration

A repaired figure is one where the entire figure is complete, but a part has been broken, and the restorer has put it back together and painted over the cracks. A restored figure is one where a piece was missing and the restorer has made up a new piece. Both repaired and restored figures should subsequently have been fired to set the enamels. By far the greater number of Staffordshire figures have either been repaired or restored or are in need of such work, and this should not be of great concern to the collector. A figure that is in its original condition is rare and will command a high price. This rare figure (see right) has an arm missing. Usually incomplete figures are not worth collecting, but as a perfect specimen would cost over £1,000/$1,600, in this case the restoration would be worthwhile.

With present-day methods, a good professional restorer's work will be almost undetectable, other than with a magnifying glass. It should be remembered that a restorer charges by the hour, and it will cost the same for a similar repair on a figure that costs £100/$160 or one that costs £1,000/$1,600.

Decoration: colouring & gilding

Underglaze cobalt blue colouring was discovered in about 1830, shortly before the introduction of the flatback, and began to be applied to Staffordshire figures. Before this discovery, there was no colour that could stand the intense heat of the glazing kiln or glost oven and remain the same. Prior to this discovery, only overglaze enamel colours, applied after glazing, were used on figures, a method that was to continue alongside the use of cobalt blue. The use of cobalt blue is a particular hallmark of the period between 1840 and 1865, and will be found on many figures of this time. After 1865, cobalt blue was only used on one or two very late figures; otherwise the overglaze enamel colours were used exclusively. The darker these enamels are, the more prone they are to flaking.

The same figure is often produced in three states: in "full colour", i.e. with underglaze and enamel colours; in "colour", i.e. with enamel colours only; or "in the white", i.e. with virtually no colour at all, other than in small details such as pink for the hands and faces, or perhaps a little black for the shoes. Full colour figures are more expensive than coloured figures, which in turn are more expensive than white figures. On all three states it is usual for gilding to be applied.

By the 1870s most figures were produced in the white, and a less expensive form of gilding was introduced, which could be painted on after the figure had been fired, thus saving time and expense. The gilding used is a good guide to dating: the early form of gilding is known as "best gold", a softly coloured gold, applied at the same time as the overglaze enamels; later gilding, "bright gold", is harsher and brassier.

Collecting tips

• Whatever category of figure you collect, it is a good idea to buy any bargain that you see. It can always be exchanged at a later date.

• Judge each figure on its merits and do not be put off by minor damage. With today's methods of repairing and restoring, you need sharp eyes to detect a good restorer's work.

• Always ask for and obtain a receipt for any purchase, and ensure that a date is given and it states if the figure has been repaired or restored.

Dogs

For many people not familiar with Staffordshire figures, dogs are the most widely recognized type. It is believed that Queen Victoria's pet King Charles spaniel, named Dash, was the inspiration for the thousands of Staffordshire dogs that were made. Known in England as "comforters", so-called because they stood on the mantelpiece and brought comfort to their surroundings, and in Scotland as "Wally Dogs", they were made in pairs to sit facing each other. They were introduced at the time of Queen Victoria's ascension to the throne in 1837, and they were so successful that hundreds of different versions were made – simple three-part moulds, more complicated figures requiring secondary moulds, figures with puppies and many different sizes.

▼ **Whippet spill vase**

Having established a popular market for spaniel figures, many other dog breeds were to follow. The most popular of these was the whippet, a small version of a greyhound and a very popular breed. This spill vase group is wonderfully constructed with a simple but effective design, and is delicately coloured. The figure is one of a pair. An extra mould, on top of the standard three-part mould, would have been required in order to make the dog's delicate head.

Spill vase of whippet chasing a rabbit, c.1850, ht 29cm/ 11½in, **£400–500/ $650–800**

Pair of whippets on cobalt blue bases, c.1865, ht 14cm/5½in, **£250–350/$400–550** (the pair)

▲ **Pair of whippets**

The most popular of the whippet figures were made in pairs, lying on oblong bases. At least ten different versions of this type are known; some have dead game lying beside the dog and some have white bases. However, most have cobalt blue bases, and they also often have a small hole on the base. This hole indicates their use as quill- or pen-holders (not inkwells as they are sometimes described).

Pair of size "2" comforters,
c.1850, ht 25.5cm/10in,
£350–450/ \$550–725 (the pair)

▲ **Pair of size "2" comforters**
This pair are the archetypal
Staffordshire figures. They are
impressed on the bottom with
size number "2", the most
common of the six impressed
sizes. They can be found in
various colour variations:
decorated in black and white
(the black was either under- or
overglaze, mostly the latter),
red and white, lustre and
white and white with gilding.
It has now become
popular to collect
all six sizes in one
particular colour; a
complete set is
very expensive.
Size "6" is the
smallest and most
difficult to find.

▼ **Spaniels with their pups**
As their popularity grew, the
potters produced a wider
variety of dog figures. Many
groups of dogs with their pups
were made; other breeds such
as poodles and game dogs were
also produced – the latter often
depicted with a rabbit or bird
in their mouth or at their feet.
Unlike portrait figures, which
had a limited appeal, the dogs
were popular for the whole
period of Staffordshire figure
production, into the 1920s.

Pricing of dog figures
The more complicated
the model, the more it is
worth. Dogs with
separate legs are more
valuable; standing dogs
are worth more than
those seated, and red and
white dogs are preferred
to those in black and
white, which are in turn
preferable to those in
white or lustre. Paired
figures are worth at least
three times the price of a
single figure, so it is
worth buying a single in
the hope of eventually
finding its pair. Dogs
with glass eyes are
always late, after 1880.

Pair of spaniels with their pups,
c.1850, ht 16.5cm/6½in,
£600–800/\$950–1,300 (the pair)

Children with dogs

Simultaneously with the introduction of the comforter (see p.10-11), the potters added sentimentality to their figures by creating pieces using the winning combination of dogs and children. The appeal of these two subjects ensured a wider market for their figures than dogs on their own could provide. A number of these figures featured the royal children of Queen Victoria and Prince Albert as they were extremely popular with the public at that time. The potters continued to make figures of children with dogs for a considerable period, and not only with dogs, but with deer, goats, sheep, horses, ponies, birds, cats and even rats. By far the best-selling type of figure, however, was a pair of a boy and a girl figure. The children can usually be found sitting on, standing beside or kneeling in front of the dog, and quite often a kennel may be included.

Spill vase: dog, girl and snake, c.1845, ht 28.5cm/11¼in, **£300–400/ $475–650**

◀ **Dog protecting a girl**
It is not unusual to find snakes on Staffordshire figures. Clearly they were a figment of the potters' imagination, as the snakes depicted have never been native to this country. They can be found attacking animals such as goats, horses, deer and wild animals or, as in this example, groups can be found where a dog is protecting a child from a snake. This group is one of a pair, the other side being almost a mirror image, with a boy asleep instead of a girl.

▼ **Girl leaning against a seated dog**
The children in this type of Staffordshire figure are always expensively dressed, often with plumed hats, and sometimes with ermine-edged clothes. Pairs of children with animals of the quality of the piece illustrated here are very desirable, and the larger the figure, the higher its value. As is often the case, there is a pair to this figure depicting a mirror image, but with a boy replacing the girl.

Girl leaning against a seated dog, c.1850, ht 20.5cm/8in, **£300–400/ $475–650**

Girl seated in chair above clock face with spaniels, c.1850, ht 30cm/ 11¾in, **£400–500/$650–800**

▲ Seated girl, above clock face, with spaniels

The potters were able to construct quite complicated figures within a simple basic design. In the example pictured above, they have managed to create a composition of two dogs, a girl holding a feeding bowl seated in a chair with her feet on a cushion, a lead on the cushion, two flags, and below it all, a clock surrounded by flowers. And all this was achieved using just three moulds – a front, a back and a base. Once again, there is a pair to this figure which is almost a mirror image, with a boy replacing the girl.

▼ Pair of figures of boy and girl with spaniels

Both coloured and uncoloured versions of the same figures were made at the same time; this was in order to appeal to the widest possible markets. On the uncoloured versions, there is usually a lot more gilding, so at the time they would not have been much less expensive than their coloured counterparts. That is no longer so, as coloured versions now always fetch more than their uncoloured counterparts. The figures shown here are each part of a separate pair, one in the white and the other in full colour.

Figures of royal children with animals

Figures depicting the children of Queen Victoria and Prince Albert are usually more expensive than merely decorative figures of unknown children with animals. Many figures purport to be of the royal children but are not. It is advisable, therefore, only to pay the premium for such portrait figures if there is a proven, identifiable source or an equivalent titled figure that has been previously recorded.

FACT FILE

Pair of figures of boy and girl seated on kennels, spaniels to the side, c.1850, ht 21.5cm/ 8½in, **£400-500/ $650-800** (coloured pair) **£200–250/ $325–400** (pair in the white)

Domestic & farmyard animals

Staffordshire potters made figures of nearly all farm animals, from cows to sheep, goats, rabbits and chickens. Horses on their own are very rare, as they are usually portrayed with their foals. Of the domestic animals produced, dog figures have been described (*see* pp.10–11), but surprisingly few models of cats were made – less than 20 as opposed to hundreds of dogs. The most common figures of cats were of a pair facing left and right, seated on a cushion, and the earliest ones, made by the Parr factory in about 1850, are very rare. The successor to the Parr family of potters was William Kent, and the moulds for many of the Parr figures were used by him between 1878 and 1962 when his factory closed. Many Parr/Kent figures are not flatbacks, but modelled and decorated in the round, distinguishing them from other makers.

▼ Crouching rabbit

At the time of writing, the record price for Victorian Staffordshire of £13,500/ $21,600 plus premium was paid at auction for a pair of recumbent rabbits eating lettuces. This was an exceptional figure and probably the result of two very determined bidders vieing for the lot, as five-figure sums are otherwise unheard of. The small rabbit illustrated here is relatively expensive for its size, but all rabbit figures are rare and therefore highly sought after.

Figure of a crouching rabbit, c.1850, ht 7.5cm/3in, **£150–200/ $250–325**

Goat being attacked by a snake, c.1855, ht 18cm/7in, **£250–350/$400–550**

◄ Goat being attacked by a snake

Figures of goats can be found in abundance, often in pairs on their own, or with attendants sitting on or standing by them. Some of the most charming figures show oversized goats towering over small children. This figure is one of a pair and the unlikely composition of a large exotic snake attacking a goat is one of which the potters were fond. The colouring in this figure is quite realistic, with a mixture of black and orange enamel paint applied with a "combed" effect.

Pair of spill vases of a ram and a ewe, in the round, c.1865, ht 14cm/5½in, **£300–400/$475–650**

▲ Pair of spill vases of a ram and a ewe

Such figures of ram and ewe spill vases, modelled in the round as opposed to with a flatback, were made by the Parr factory for many years, and later Kent versions from 1880 can also be found. All Staffordshire figures have a small hole, either in the back or in the base, which was to allow the hot air to escape when the figure was fired in the kiln. If, however, the figure is a spill vase, as illustrated here, or a quill holder, this small hole was not necessary as the vases incorporated an opening anyway. This pair of figures was also produced at the larger size of 20.5cm/8in.

▼ Pair of cats on cushions

This pair of cats was made in the Kent factory in about 1890. Wiliam Kent either acquired or bought the Parr factory moulds, including such moulds of cat figures. Cats are very rare among Staffordshire figures and much in demand. The earlier Parr cats can be told apart from the Kent versions by the quality of the decoration (see Fact File). Due to their rarity cat figures have often been reproduced, and great care should be taken when purchasing, as moulds have been taken from genuine figures. Early Parr pairs now fetch over £2,000/$3,200.

Parr & Kent factories

Thomas Parr was in production from 1852 to 1870; from then until 1879 the factory was in the control of John Parr. He went into partnership with William Kent in 1880 and the pottery became known as Kent & Parr until it changed to William Kent in 1894.

Parr figures can be distinguished from Kent figures by the colouring and decoration. The early Parr figures are painted in delicate green and brown, applied with a "combed" effect. From 1880, the paint becomes darker and is coated not combed on.

Pair of cats seated on cushions, c.1890, ht 19.5cm/7¾in, **£1,000–1,500/$1.600–2,400** (the pair)

Wild animals

The range of wild animals made by the Staffordshire potters would do justice to a small zoo. Rarities include a figure of a rhinoceros, which forms the lid of a tureen and is part of an extremely rare dinner service that also includes a leopard and an elephant. Considering that the potters would have had little opportunity of studying most of these animals, and that any first-hand knowledge would probably have been limited to viewing them at a circus or travelling menagerie, the resulting representations are quite superb in their accuracy. This quality has now been recognized in the marketplace, as the prices being obtained for these figures are amongst the highest for any Staffordshire figures. For later, less expensive wild animals, *see* p.57.

Figure of standing zebra, c.1850, ht 16cm/6¼in, **£280–350/ $450–550**

▼ Standing zebra
Like the animals in the ark that went in two by two, most of the Staffordshire animal figures were made in pairs, and this standing figure of a zebra is no exception. The early figures of zebras, from about 1845, were actually horses with stripes painted on them, but shortly thereafter, around 1850, correctly modelled figures of zebras appeared, as pictured left. This figure can also be found as a 25.5cm/10in version, which is more expensive: over £1,000/$1,600 per pair has been paid for that size.

▲ Standing zebra/horse
An incorrectly modelled figure of a zebra, this is a horse with stripes painted on, and an identical figure has been found which is decorated as a horse. It clearly has a horse's mane, and the reins are evident. The potter had the horse mould in stock and produced a zebra from it to save time and money.

Standing zebra/ horse, c.1845, ht 21.5cm/8½in, **£300–350/ $475–550**

▼ Spill vase figure of a standing lion

The pair to this figure is a mirror image, as is usual in Staffordshire figures. Lions were just one of the many wild animals made by the potters: others include stags and does, elephants, foxes, giraffes, gorillas, monkeys, leopards, tigers and squirrels. This particular model is one of those found by divers in the ship that sunk off the Kent coast in 1853 (see below).

Spill vase of a standing lion, c.1850, ht 17cm/6¾in, **£400–500/$650–800**

Death of a "Lion Queen"
The famous death of a female lion tamer, Ellen Bright, from an attack by a tiger was depicted in a figure of which two versions exist, one of which is titled "The Death of a Lion Queen". Her death caused the law to change: thereafter only men were allowed to become lion tamers.

Figure of lion attacking a stag, c.1860, ht 16.5cm/6½in, **£400–500/$650–800**

▲ Lion attacking a stag

The potters were fond of portraying animals in extremis, and groups can be found of leopards attacking deer, dogs attacking or chasing stags, lions bringing down deer or zebra, and snakes coiled around all manner of animals. All such figures are highly sought after and very collectable. Animal figures were also exported. A ship bound for America that had sunk off the Kent coast in 1853 was salvaged by divers over 140 years later, and Staffordshire figures were found, including figures of lions and elephants. The only water damage was to the colour.

Spill vase of fox with dead bird, c.1850, ht 24cm/9½in, **£280–350/$450–550**

▲ Spill vase of fox with bird

This figure is another example of the popular tradition of producing figures of animals hunting and killing one another, something that was not considered cruel but part of nature. This figure is currently being reproduced in the Far East and care should be taken to ensure that it is an original.

Occupations

The Victorian period was a time of social upheaval; England was changing from being a mainly rural economy and turning to industrial occupations. Workers, needed in the factories, were leaving the countryside for the towns. The potters, eager to increase their market, made figures of the occupations left behind by these rural workers. Many figures were idealized versions of the truth, but they had a nostalgia that made them desirable, a reminder of what had been lost. A wide range of subjects were potted: farmers, milkmen and milkmaids, water carriers, harvesters, bakers, flower sellers and so on. The occupations of townsfolk were not so popular and few figures of this type were made, although there is one of a "crossing sweeper" (a boy who swept the road for gentry to cross), three blacksmiths, a fireman and a paper seller.

▶ **Gypsy fortune-teller**
The gypsies who travelled the length and breadth of the kingdom earned a living by telling people's fortunes, either at their houses or at the many fairs held on religious and public holidays. The potters captured these scenes in clay, and whether they were intended to be bought by the gypsy, the public or both is not known. It is probable that the figures were sold at the fairs or markets where the gypsies worked and were taken home as a reminder of a pleasant day. Here the young woman is paying the gypsy, or "crossing her palm with silver".

Spill vase of gypsy fortune-teller, c.1850, ht 24cm/9½in, £180–250/ $300–400

▼ **Spill vase of gypsy fortune-teller**
Another version of a gypsy fortune-teller: in this figure the gypsy is reading a girl's palm. It is possible that figures such as these had a theatrical inspiration or source. This figure was made by the Parr factory, and is very well modelled and decorated all around, as is typical of this factory. Hundreds of brush-strokes have been applied to form the dresses of the girl and the gypsy.

Spill vase of a gypsy fortune-teller, c.1850, ht 32cm/12½in, £180–250/ $300–400

Collecting tips
Figures depicting occu-
pations is an area which
at present is under-
collected and bargains
can still be found. Many
of the figures are very
well modelled and
decorated, but until
recently few have been
recorded or catalogued.

Gardener and his family, c.1850, ht
24cm/9½in, **£180–250/$300–400**

▲ Gardener and his family
Most of the occupations
portrayed related to the
countryside and gardeners
were a very popular subject.
The figure of a proud gardener,
holding a spade and a basket
of fruit he has just harvested,
with his wife and child beside
him, was an idealized country
scene. The reality was that in
the countryside the work
hours were long and the
wages low. The "Truck Act",
whereby employers could pay
their workers in goods and not
money, caused much hardship.

"The Gardener", c.1850, ht 28cm/
11in, **£400–500/$650–800**

▲ "The Gardener"
Many other gardening figures
similar to this one can be found
but very few are titled: there is
only one of this particular figure
known, titled or untitled. It
came to light only recently in
a small collection – it had been
bought many years previously
but the collector was unaware
of its rarity. Few titled figures are
unrecorded and, when they do
appear, they are highly prized.

▼ Milkman and milkmaid
On later Staffordshire figures
such as this, the potters eco-
nomized on the decoration:
instead of using a "feathering"
technique to apply colour, the
paint was applied in a solid
coat, creating a harsher effect.
The decoration of the dresses
and skirts of earlier versions,
which had involved hundreds
of tiny brush strokes, became
one solid colour. In this pair of
milkman and milkmaid figures
with their cows, the modelling
is still very good, but the quality
of the decoration is not what it
was ten or twenty years before.
These figures are still very
collectable, but the earlier
versions will be more expensive.

Pair of cows with milkman and
milkmaid c.1870, ht 21.5cm/8½in,
£600–700/$950–1,125 (the pair)

Shepherds & fishermen

Whilst most rural occupations were potted into figures, by far the greatest number of these were of shepherds and shepherdesses. Figures of pastoral scenes had been made long before the Victorian period by such potters as Walton, Wood, Caldwell, Sherratt and others. Many of them were inscribed with titles such as "Rural Pastimes", "Lost Sheep Found", "Shepherd" and "Shepherdess", and the inspiration for a number of these pastoral figures was adapted copies of pre-Victorian figures. Another popular occupation to pot was fishing as, being an island nation, there were fishing communities all around the coasts of Britain, to whom the potters supplied a variety of figures. The flatback was a strong feature of Victorian Staffordshire work, and its innovative simplicity is seen to best effect in these titled rural scenes.

Spill vase of "Welsh Shepherds", c.1855, ht 33.5cm/13¼in, **£300–350/ $475–550**

▼ **Spill vase figure "Welsh Shepherds"**
This figure of "Welsh Shepherds" is an example of how the potters expanded and targeted a particular market by including a title on the piece. Without the title the figure would have been an attractive decorative ornament; with the title it was also made desirable to the numerous Welsh shepherds and farmers who lived not far from Staffordshire. This figure is in full colour, and as a spill vase it was useful for standing on the mantelpiece and holding the rolled-up pieces of paper that substituted the then much more expensive matches.

▶ **Standing shepherd**
This figure of a standing shepherd with his crook is also a spill vase. His dog and a sheep complete the group. Whilst this figure is in "colour", it is not in "full colour", as no underglaze cobalt blue has been used. This figure was originally one of a pair, but over the course of time its partner has either been lost or broken. After 1865, the use of underglaze blue virtually ceased, and neither this figure nor its pair has ever been recorded with under-glaze blue colouring. This allows an approximate dating for this figure of after 1865.

Spill vase of standing shepherd, c.1865, ht 25.5cm/10in, **£200–250/ $325–400**

▼ Seated shepherdess

What is interesting about this shepherdess is that she is holding a book. Today that would be of little consequence, but in 1860 illiteracy was common, particularly amongst rural communities, and more so with girls than boys. It would have been a source of amazement to many that a girl could read. This piece is an adaptation of figures made in the early 1800s by John Walton and by Martha Sherratt entitled "Reading Maid".

Seated shepherdess with sheep, c.1860, ht 18.5cm/7¼in, **£150–200/$250–325**

Group figure of fisherman and his family, c.1850, ht 28cm/11in, **£300–400/$475–650**

▲ Fisherman and his family

Fishing in Britain was an industry that employed many thousands of people, and the potters ensured that figures of fishermen, fisherwomen and fish sellers were produced to meet this potential market. The figure of the fisherman and his family is large and would have been complicated to pot; he sits in the boat casting his net with the child standing on his wife's lap; a basket of fish floats on the sea. All this is achieved using just the standard three moulds, a front, back and base.

Standing fisherman, c.1855, ht 35.5cm/14in, **£300–350/$475–550**

▲ Standing fisherman

This figure is very well modelled and decorated, his waistcoat alone having nearly 120 brushstrokes to create the pattern. The figure is painted except for the base, which is white with a gilded line. The sharp features and details suggest it is early from the mould. Its perfect condition makes it very desirable.

Hunters

Hunting as a sport or merely as a means of providing food was extremely popular in Victorian times. The wealthy would hunt deer and shoot grouse; falconry was prevalent and the fox hunt was a countrywide pursuit. Farmers would also shoot foxes, badgers, otters and rabbits to clear their land of what they considered as pests, and most animals were considered fair game. Cock fighting and the setting of terriers onto rats in a pit were widespread sports, and substantial betting would take place. The poor man could not afford a gun, and poaching, while dangerous, could feed hungry families so many men kept a whippet – a small greyhound, which could be let loose on the gentry's land to bring home a rabbit for the pot. The figures that potters produced depicting these pursuits and pastimes were bought by rich and poor alike.

▶ **Standing figure of a hunter with his dog**
A number of the figures of this type made showed hunters dressed in unusual clothes, more theatrical than was actually the case. This figure of a hunter standing with a dog by his side, a rifle in his hand and a dead bird at his feet is a perfect example of this. He wears an unusual style of cap, a long ermine-edged cape, a jacket with tassles, knee-length breeches and ankle boots. It is possible, in view of the style of their clothing, that this and the figure shown opposite were both inspired by a theatrical source.

Standing figure of a hunter with his dog, c.1850, ht 36cm/14¼in, **£300–400/ $475–650**

▼ **Standing figure of a falconer with his dog**
The figure of a hunter with his dog, shown left, must have been a reasonably popular figure, for a similar figure group is shown here. Whilst the dress is almost the same as that worn by the hunter, the hat has been changed and the figure appears as a falconer with a bird aloft. Both of these figures are in "full colour", that is, using underglaze blue as well as enamel colours, but they are also found in the white with very little colour.

Falconer with dog, c.1850, ht 38cm/15in, **£300–400/$475–650**

▼ Scottish hunter with dog

Many of the figures of hunters were dressed in Highland garb, complete with a sporran, and a substantial collection of these figures alone could be made. In this figure, the highlander is kneeling on a grassy bank, one hand on his dog's head, the other holding a dead stag aloft by its hind legs. The base shape of this figure is known as "Rococo" and the potter has gone to the trouble of shaping and scrolling it. Rococo bases are not uncommon on Staffordshire figures, and were made over a considerable period.

Seated Scottish hunter with dog and dead stag, c.1860, ht 28.5cm/ 11¼in, **£300–400/$475–650**

▼ Spill vase of Scottish hunter with dog

Almost a cross between the figure on the far left and the one to the immediate left is this spill vase figure. The hunter wears a plumed hat, a short jacket, an ermine-edged cloak and a skirt; the dog is posed similarly to the previous figure and the man holds a gun in the crook of his arm. As in the figure on the far left, a dead bird lies on the base. It is still a mystery as to why so many figures of strangely dressed huntsmen were made: none are titled so if they were made to represent a particular person or character the identity has been lost, probably forever.

Price of hunting figures

These figures have sold for less than comparable portrait pieces because until recently they have not been fully recorded. (See p.61 for details of A. & N. Harding's book with its complete catalogue.) At present, many still offer good value.

FACT FILE

▼ Pair of standing hunters

It is unusual for pairs to be of the same sex; this pair have been taken to represent Robin Hood and Little John. However, great care should be taken in accepting that unnamed figures are of particular persons, as this is often done to enhance the value of a figure. It may be right here, though, as this pair bears strong similarity to a figure of two men entitled "Robin Hood". Here they are on Rococo bases.

Pair of standing hunters, c.1875, ht 26cm/10¼in, **£300–400/$475–650**

Spill vase of Scottish hunter with dog, c.1865, ht 33cm/13in, **£200–250/$325–400**

Decorative figures

By definition, decorative figures are those that are not Portraits, Military, Theatrical or Religious figures, but were produced purely as decorative ornaments with no other purpose, usually depicting pastoral scenes. Many decorative figures have a source or inspiration, and the finding of such a source is not just satisfying, it can also appreciate the value of a figure. Illustrations in the form of prints or engravings, from newspapers and music sheets, were used and adapted, as were a number of woolwork pictures. The Great Exhibition of 1851 at London's Crystal Palace contained sculptures that became the basis for several figures, as did paintings at London's Royal Academy. But by far the greatest number of figures originated in the potter's or modeller's own imagination, and were none the less appealing for that. It was the modeller who was the true artist as he made the figure for the moulds.

Boy seated on gate with girl behind, c.1870, ht 19cm/7½in, **£250–350/ $400–550**

▼ Boy seated on a gate with a girl standing behind

This figure of a boy on a gate is one which has a found and proven source. In 1836, William Collins R.A. exhibited a painting at the Royal Academy's Summer Exhibition entitled *Happy as a King*. In 1869, it was made into a popular print, and this figure is taken from the painting or print. It is probable that the potter saw a copy of the print in 1869 and sourced his figure from that, as the figure certainly does not date back as early as 1836.

▼ Two boys carrying a girl over a stream

This figure of two boys and a girl has a similar source to that of the boy and girl left. In 1842, William Mulready R.A. exhibited a painting at the Royal Academy entitled *Crossing the Brook* (now hanging in London's Tate Gallery), and this figure is taken from that work. It is not known for certain when prints were made from the painting, but the figure dates from c.1865. It is unlikely that the potter saw the original, and much more probable that he used one of these prints as his source.

Two boys carrying a girl, c.1865, ht 25.5cm/10in, **£250–350/ $400–550**

"The Travellers" – woman and girl seated on a horse, c.1855, ht 25.5cm/10in, **£400–500/$650–800**

◀ **"The Travellers"**
Gypsies commonly travelled the length and breadth of the country in the mid 19thC. This figure is in full colour, with underglaze blue used, albeit sparingly, on the blouses of the gypsy and child. No less than eight enamel colours make up the palette, and the best gold gilding has been used to highlight the blouses and line the base. It is early from the mould, with sharp features, noticeable particularly in the woman's sharply delineated fingers. This is one of a rare and valuable pair: the other has a gypsy man with a boy seated on a horse.

▼ **"Orange Sellers"**
Some figures are always titled and some are never titled. There are also figures that have both titled and untitled versions, and the "Orange Sellers" falls into this category. The presence of a title in such cases, as here, will increase the value of the figure. The clay used in the production of Staffordshire figures was always very white, and this light background was used to great effect by the potters to highlight certain parts of the figure, as is demonstrated in the woman's shawl on this figure.

"Orange Sellers", c.1870, ht 34.5cm/ 13½in, **£200–250/ $325–400**

Tracing the source of a figure
If a source can be found for a decorative figure, identifying it as a portrait or theatrical piece, its value increases. The reverse is also true: some figures have doubtful attributions that, if wrong, may decrease their value.

"Rival", c.1855, ht 30.5cm/12in, **£450–550/$725–875**

▲ **"Rival" – an arbour group**
The Rivals, a comedy by R. B. Sheridan, was first performed in 1775 and was clearly popular in Victorian times, as there are at least six different versions of this figure, some titled, some not. Until the discovery of this figure in 1999, all versions were thought to be decorative only; they have now been transformed into valuable theatrical figures.

Inexpensive decorative figures

Many smaller Staffordshire figures were produced very cheaply in their thousands, often to be given away at fairs as prizes, known as "fairings". The quality of these figures varies: some are badly decorated; some are hardly decorated at all; and on some the moulds were used so many times that only inferior figures could emerge. However, there are finer small decorative figures to be found – the ones to look for are those that are early from the mould, for these have sharper features and are usually better decorated, in full colour with underglaze blue. The figures have a naive charm that makes them highly collectable and many have a pastoral or rustic theme. The figures from around 1830, decorated and modelled in the round, are superior to 1840–70 pieces.

▶ **Spill vase of man, woman and sheep**
This spill vase figure is decorated in full colour: underglaze blue has been used on his jacket and her blouse, and the rest of the figure has been decorated using three enamel colours, black, orange and green. The potters saved on gilding by using a yellow line on the base. An added decoration is incorporated in the clumps of grass applied to the figure: the method used for this was to pass the clay through a sieve and attach it to the figure before firing. The figure has suffered some damage: there is a hairline crack and a chip to the base, and the noses of the group have been scuffed. In perfect condition, it would be worth £100/$160.

Spill vase of man, woman and sheep, c.1860, ht 20.5cm/8in, **£50–75/$75–125**

▼ **Boy and girl harvesters**
This figure of a boy and girl holding wheatsheaves, standing on either side of a clockface, is in full colour and is competently constructed. Sieved clay has been used on the base and, on this occasion, the potter has applied a gilded line to the base. The figure is perfect – there are no chips, cracks or repairs to decrease its value.

Boy and girl with wheatsheaves, c.1860, ht 19cm/7½in, **£40–60/$75–100**

▼ Man and woman with fruit and garlands

This group figure of a couple shows the man standing and the woman seated, both holding garlands. The potter's palette was not very extensive, and if underglaze blue was used then usually only four other enamel colours, including black, completed the decoration, for reasons of economy. The figure illustrated here is of average standard, but on the better-decorated figures there can be literally hundreds of small brush strokes making up the design or pattern on a dress.

Man and woman with fruit and garlands, c.1855, ht 16.5cm/6½in, **£40–50/$65–75**

Arbour group of boy and girl with bird's nest, c.1860, ht 20.5cm/8in, **£60–80/$100–125**

▲ Arbour group of boy and girl with bird's nest

Many arbour figures were produced by the Staffordshire potters. In this example, a bird's nest, complete with eggs, rests in the arbour above the man's and woman's head. A separate mould has been used for the bird that is perched on the man's knee. No less than six enamel colours have been used on this figure, and there is also some gilding, but there is no underglaze blue which might give a clue as to its date.

Girl with bird and harp, c.1855, ht 23cm/9in, **£100–125/$160–200**

▲ Girl with bird and harp

The long scarf worn by this girl denotes that she is probably a dancer. It is generally possible to ascertain if a figure is one of a pair: the pair to this is a man in a similar pose, but he holds a mandolin, with a dog by his side. The common factors that help to identify them as a pair are the gate and the bird.

Titled theatrical figures

This is a field that in the past has been very well researched as a number of early Staffordshire collectors were either connected with or had an interest in the theatre. When a theatrical figure is titled, its origin is obvious, but it has also been customary among collectors to attribute the name of the actor who performed the role at the time the figure was made. This is unnecessary and erroneous, as the actor would have been known to hardly anyone at the time, and it may well have restricted the sales of the figure if their identity was emphasised. The potters chose not to put the artist's name on the figure, one exception being a figure of the "Misses Cushman in Character of Romeo & Juliet", where the dramatic moment being portrayed was most important.

◀ "Othello & Iago"

Most titled theatrical figures were sourced from engravings or prints, and this figure is no exception. In 1858, an engraving of a watercolour by S. A. Hart R.A. of this subject appeared in *The National Magazine*, and the potters adapted the figure from this engraving. The use of black script on raised titling is usually an indication that the figure is a second: some damage had probably occurred during production so black enamel was used rather than more expensive gilding.

"Othello & Iago", c.1860, ht 30.5cm/12in, **£800–1,000/ $1,300–1,600**

▼ "Winter's Tale" spill vase

One of the earliest sources discovered for this figure was a series of engravings by Tallis published in book form in 1852, entitled *Shakespeare Gallery*. They were later republished by the London Printing Company Ltd under the title *William Shakespeare's Works*. These engravings were used by at least two potters as a source for their figures. The Parr factory made more than seven of the Tallis engravings into figures, and this Winter's Tale piece is one of that number. It is the only figure, however, that was made as a spill vase.

Spill vase of "Winter's Tale", c.1855, ht 30.5cm/12in, **£350–450/ $550–725**

Sources of titled theatrical figures

Over the years, many publications have been searched for sources. It is unlikely that any more discoveries will be made in *The Illustrated London News*, as this has now been thoroughly researched. However, some sources may still be found in Victorian prints and engravings, or in music fronts (the illustrated front page of a piece of sheet music) from between the years of 1840 and 1870.

▼ Pair of figures of "D. Turpin" and "Tom King"

The pair of figures of Dick Turpin and Tom King were very popular pieces: over thirteen different versions were made by a number of diverse potters, mostly showing them facing each other riding a horse, as pictured here, though two standing pairs without horses can also be found. Whilst Turpin and King were historical figures, and it was widely known that Turpin had shot and killed King by mistake (a crime for which he was hanged in 1739) it is likely that these figures were based on the melodramas produced during Victorian times, one of which appeared at the Theatre Royal in London in 1841.

Standing figure of "Falstaff", c.1855, ht 24cm/9½in, **£250–350/$400–550**

▲ "Falstaff"

Falstaff was another of the figures sourced from the Tallis engravings by the Parr factory. Like the others, it is modelled and coloured all around. Parr had a very distinctive form of titling, using indented capitals almost like printers' type that were then coloured with black enamel or gilded, as seen here. Another identifiable Parr feature is that they rarely used underglaze blue on their figures. A smaller 17cm/6¾in version of this figure was also made.

Pair of figures of Dick Turpin and Tom King, c.1850, ht 24cm/9½in, **£450–550/ $725–875** (the pair)

Theatrical figures

The theatre was the source for a number of Staffordshire figures, and in an age before radio or television, it was a very popular form of entertainment for rich and poor alike. It was not just straight theatre with its innumerable Shakespeare productions – melodramas where the audience could shout their displeasure at the villain and cheer the hero were also very popular, as were the travelling fairs and menageries. Astley's circus, for example, which was a cross between a circus and a melodrama, held in a circus-type ring, performed to full houses from all over the country. It is possible that figures were sold at these places of popular entertainment as a reminder of the performance. Van Amburgh the lion tamer, a keen publicist, commissioned two versions of figures of himself, titled eponymously, that were doubtless sold at his shows.

▶ **Romeo and Juliet**
An exception to the rule of titled theatrical figures (see pp.28–29), no source for this figure is known, but the pose and other similarities to titled figures of Romeo and Juliet are such that this may safely be assumed to be a representation of the tragic Shakespeare lovers. It is quite a rare figure, titled or untitled, and, when found, is always sparsely coloured. It is not known which factory made this figure. It is an early piece, c.1850, modelled in the round with extra moulds, and has an unusual stepped base, not seen on many figures.

Romeo and Juliet, c.1850, ht 28.5cm/ 11¼in, **£500– 600/$800–950**

Man in a tent, c.1860, ht 16.5cm/6½in, **£60–80/$95–130**

▼ **Man seated in tent**
This figure can be found in at least three sizes. Not only has the source been traced, but the largest figure is titled "Richard the Third". This large version, measuring 24cm/9½in, is better modelled than the smaller ones: over £500/$800 has been paid for it in perfect condition. The source was a 1745 painting, The Nightmare Scene by William Hogarth, which was later engraved. The original hangs in the Walker Art Gallery in Liverpool.

Theatrical attributions
Like their portrait counterparts, many figures of this style have been given rather dubious theatrical attributions, which may decrease the figure's value if proven to be incorrect. It is also considered unwise to pay the premium for a theatrical figure that has no known source or titled equivalent.

▼ Female jockey

This figure was made in the early 1830s, evident in its being modelled in the round. Its source is a "penny plain and tuppence coloured print" (prints sold for a penny if black and white, or for tuppence [two pennies] if coloured in). Illustrated here with the figure, the print is inscribed "Miss Foote as 'The Little Jockey'" – a comic opera performed at the Olympic Theatre in London in 1831. The figure pre-dates the use of underglaze blue and is decorated only with underglaze enamel colours.

Female jockey holding a whip, c.1835, ht 16cm/6¼in, **£350–450/$550–725**

Actor Edward Sothern, c.1860, ht 21.5cm/8½in, **£400–500/$650–800**

▲ Figure of actor Edward Sothern

Little-known English actor, Edward Sothern, played the part of Lord Dundreary in a play entitled *Our American Cousin*. It was first performed on Broadway in New York in 1859. The part of Dundreary, originally a minor one, was expanded by Sothern with much success, and when the play came to England in 1861 it was even more popular. The source of the figure was the music front of the *Lord Dundreary Waltz*. Sothern became closely identified with the part; illustrated with the figure is this contemporary photograph of the actor.

Mr Van Amburgh with lions, c.1840, ht 16cm/6¼in, **£2,000–3,000/$3,200–4,800**

▲ "Mr Van Amburgh"

Isaac Van Amburgh first brought his lion-taming act from the USA to England in 1838. Dressed as a gladiator, he performed in a cage with lions, leopards and lambs, making the lion lie down with the lamb. Two versions of this rare figure exist: the tamer with lions and a lion cub, or lions and a lamb.

Dancers & musicians

The range and quantity of figures of dancers and musicians produced was prodigious. The potters occasionally portrayed particular people or events, but most simply gave free range to their imaginations. Many of the figures were made in pairs, others were made to stand alone. Some of the group figures of this type were among the largest Staffordshire figures made: the largest recorded figure, a portrait figure of Napoleon Bonaparte, is 61cm/24in high, and it is not unusual to find figure groups measuring 45.5-60cm/18-20in. Some figures appear to be of theatrical origin, but many were of the itinerant travelling musicians and dancers. These figures were rarely made to portray a particular person, but a few did have sources that have been lost. If found, they can transform a decorative figure into a more valuable theatrical figure.

◀ **Figure of a man holding a scarf**

This figure is dressed in a theatrical costume. He holds a scarf, which nearly always denotes a dancer; this is also indicated here by the man's legs being crossed in a dancing pose. The figure is one of a pair made by quite a prolific modeller whose work can be readily identified by the vibrant green bases and slightly oriental features of his figures. It is most common for a pair to be one male and one female, so the pair for this figure would be of a woman dancing. It is possible that somewhere a source exists, or once existed, for figures such as these: if found and identified, the source would enhance their value considerably.

Man holding a scarf, c.1855, ht 24cm/9½in, **£200–250/ $325–400**

▶ **Man and woman dancing**

This dancing group is almost certainly of theatrical origin; there are a number of versions of the same figure. The likely source was a ballet, *Catarina ou La Fille du Brigand*, which was performed in 1846 at Her Majesty's Theatre, London. Jules Perrot played the part of Diavolino, and Lucille Grahn the part of Catarina. A music front exists, from which a similar group was sourced.

Dancing man and woman, c.1850, ht 25cm/9¾in, **£200–250/ $325–400**

Dancing girls with scarf, c.1850, ht 25cm/9¾in, **£200–250/$325–400**

▲ **Dancing girls with scarf**
This figure is also of dancers in theatrical costume performing with a scarf. They are probably performing a version of the polka. This dance was very popular during the mid to late 1840s, sparked by the publication by French impresario and conductor Antoine Louis Jullien in 1844 of a series of *Celebrated Polkas*, which included "The Opera Polka" and "The Queen & Prince Albert Polka". The trend inspired other polka figures to be made.

▼ **Pair of musicians**
By the style of their dress, it appears that this pair of musicians, the man playing a harp and the woman a mandolin, are not theatrical but probably represent a pair of itinerant musicians. Measuring 30.5cm/12in, they make a splendid pair. The bases are decorated with a fruiting grape vine, an unusual feature that adds to the appeal of the figures. It is very difficult to find pairs of this quality and size, and this particular pair are "matched", that is they are not a true pair but have been found separately and put together by a collector.

Pair of musicians, c.1860, ht 30.5cm/12in, **£600–700/ $950–1,100**

Production numbers
There is no such thing as a limited edition: no one knows how many pieces of a particular figure were made. Many figures are rare now because they did not sell well and no more were produced – often only one or two copies are recorded. Any later versions are considered as reproductions.

Two musicians, c.1865, ht 30.5cm/ 12in, **£300–400/$475–650**

▲ **Group figure of musicians**
This figure, which is in perfect condition, is a product of the Parr Factory. It is modelled and decorated in the round and, whilst coloured all over, no underglaze blue has been used, both of which are characteristic Parr features. A well-constructed piece, two extra moulds were used for the legs.

Royalty

The ascension of Queen Victoria to the throne in 1837 heralded a new era in production and design; potters took full advantage of the simpler production methods that followed the invention of the flatback design. Many figures of Queen Victoria and Prince Albert were produced, both as pairs and, later, with their children. When Albert died in 1861, the potters concentrated on the royal children, who were at that time entering adulthood and approaching marriage; figures of the royal princes were made throughout their childhood and when taking their commissions in the Army and Navy. Pieces were also produced on the announcement of all the royal marriages. Production ran into the 20thC, the last figures being of Edward VII and Queen Alexandra in 1901.

◀ **Queen Victoria and Prince Albert with the royal children**
Figures of Victoria and Albert with their children were a very popular subject and many versions were produced, including figures such as these, showing the proud parents seated with their children at their side. This particular pair illustrated are the finest of their type produced. The underglaze and overglaze enamels are very delicately applied and the King and Queen's ermine-edged cloaks were made by passing clay through a sieve and then applying it after the mould had dried.

Victoria, Albert and children, c.1840, ht 18cm/7in, **£600–700/$950–1,100**

▼ **Seated figure of Queen Victoria**
This figure shows Queen Victoria dressed in an ermine-edged cloak and seated on a circular, gilt-lined base, with her foot resting on a cushion. No figure of Prince Albert has ever been recorded that pairs with it, though this is not so unusual as there are a number of figures of Victoria that do not have a pair. It is quite probable, therefore, that no pair was ever made for this figure as it may just pre-date the marriage of Queen Victoria to Prince Albert in 1840.

Seated figure of Queen Victoria, c.1840, ht 18.5cm/7¼in, **£350–450/$550–725**

"Matching" figures

Very often over the last 150 years one of a pair of figures has been lost or broken. It is possible to find a pair to a single figure and "match" them. It is however difficult to find a good "match" as the decoration is likely to be different: on a true pair the colours on the base would be identical, but on a "matched" pair these colours may differ.

▼ Queen Victoria and Prince Albert standing beneath an umbrella

This figure is quite unusual – very few versions depicting Albert and Victoria standing under an umbrella were ever made. It is not known for certain if there is any great significance to the umbrella, but many of the potter's sources came from music fronts, and it is possible that this figure is in fact one of theatrical inspiration, which has been adapted to suit a market calling for figures of the royal family.

▼ Queen Victoria, holding a baby, and Prince Albert

With untitled pairs of figures such as these it is not possible to determine whom of the royal children is portrayed. It is more than probable that figures were made to commemorate the birth of each of Victoria and Albert's children. These figures are particularly well modelled and coloured; it appears that Prince Albert is holding either a coin or a biscuit in his hand.

Victoria and baby, and Albert, c.1840, ht 16.5cm/6½in, **£350–450/$550–725**

▼ Queen Victoria on a horse

This is a fine figure of Victoria on horseback, although the tail is missing. The figure pairs with one of Albert on a horse and the probable source is a coloured engraving of Victoria inspecting the troops. An inferior pair exists with Victoria's headscarf omitted and no separate moulds for the horse's legs. The figure can also be found at 19cm/7½in.

Victoria on a horse, c.1850, ht 23cm/9in, **£350–450/$550–725**

Victoria and Albert beneath an umbrella, c.1840, ht 20.5cm/8in, **£250–300/$400–475**

Victoria and Albert
on horses, c.1855, ht
20.5cm/8in, **£500–
600/$800–950**

Princess Royal and Prince
of Wales in a cart, c.1845,
ht 19cm/7½in, **£850–950/
$1,350–1,500**

Princess Royal on a pony,
c.1845, ht 18cm/7in,
£250–300/$400–475

▲ **Princess Royal and
Prince of Wales in
a pony-driven cart**
This figure, titled
"Prince and Princess",
is unusual in having a
flower basket, as well
as the figures, in the
carriage. Also very rare is
a version with a small spaniel
seated in the same position as
the flower basket, which can
be found in two sizes, 18cm/7in
and 21cm/8¼in. The wheel of
the carriage is not separate,
being moulded into the figure.
There is another version that
shows a goat pulling the
carriage instead of a pony.

▲ **Queen Victoria and
Prince Albert on horseback**
Figures such as these were a
popular theme, with over fifteen
different versions recorded. Of
all the recorded figures of
Victoria and Albert produced,
it is interesting to note that
only a handful of figures were
ever titled. This is undoubtedly
because such an addition would
have been deemed unnecessary.
Very similar, but titled, pairs of
figures were made of Sir Robert
Sale (Commander of the British
retreat at Kabul) and his wife.

▲ **Princess Royal
on a pony**
This figure pairs
with the Prince
of Wales. Many
figures of the young
children on ponies were
made in the potteries, and
their production carried on for
a number of years. It is also
possible to find similar versions
titled in gilt script. With many
versions on the market of
figures of young children with
ponies, care should be taken
when considering a purchase,
as many are erroneously attributed as royal children. To help
identify the royal figures, the
Prince of Wales always wears a
three-feathered hat, and the girls
are usually riding side-saddle.

Collectability of royals
Royalty is one of the most collected categories of Staffordshire figures in Great Britain. There is a huge range of figures, from Queen Victoria and Prince Albert, to the royal children from birth through to marriage. The majority of these pieces are of the highest quality.

Prince of Wales and Princess Alexandra of Denmark, c.1863, ht 39.5cm/15½in, **£350–450/$550–725**

▲ **"Prince & Princess"**
This figure was issued to commemorate the marriage of Edward, Prince of Wales, to Princess Alexandra of Denmark on 10 March 1863. This figure is titled "Prince & Princess" – the smaller, 24cm/9½in version uses "and" instead of an ampersand. There are also two other versions: one is a pair, identical to the figure illustrated except that there are two separate figures; the second, titled or untitled and in three sizes, is reversed with the Prince on the left and the Princess holding a bonnet on her left arm.

Princess Louise and Duke of Argyll, c.1871, ht 28.5cm/11¼in, **£250–300/$400–475**

▲ **Princess Louise and the Duke of Argyll**
This figure also commemorates a marriage, that of Princess Louise to John Douglas Sutherland Campbell, 9th Duke of Argyll, in 1871. Louise was the last of Victoria's children to be married of whom figures were produced, and the date these figures were made is reflected in their quality. They are sparsely coloured and the modelling is not up to the standard of the earlier figures. There are other versions of this figure with even less colouring, and one measuring 23cm/9in.

"Napoleon & Albert", c.1854, ht 28cm/11in, **£500–600/$800–950**

▲ **Titled figure of Napoleon III and Prince Albert**
The Crimean War (1854–56) saw the alliance of England, Turkey and France against the Russians and proved a popular source of inspiration for potters. This figure also comes at 19cm/7½in. Many similar versions were made using four different models in varying sizes.

Portrait figures

The potters took great pride in their portrait figures, and these account for some of the finest pieces of Victorian Staffordshire produced. The scope of the different portraits was immense: just over 100 different personalities have been recorded, most of whom were made in a number of varying models. The people that were potted range from the military commanders and naval admirals of the time (notably during the Crimean War of 1854-56), Prime Ministers and famous members of parliament, poets (both living and dead), clergymen, foreign dignitaries, notorious murderers and other famous historical and contemporary figures. Many collectors choose to collect a single theme, such as the Crimean War or political figures. Each theme is personal to each collector, but with the keen collector, it is mostly the Staffordshire figures themselves that hold the appeal, rather than the history behind them.

Benjamin Franklin, c.1850, ht 25.5cm/10in, **£350–400/ $550–650**

▼ **Benjamin Franklin**
The philosopher and statesman Benjamin Franklin (1706–90), was the American representative in England for eighteen years. On returning to his homeland he played a major part in drafting the Constitution and was one of only five men to sign the Declaration of Independence in 1776. American politicians were quite a popular subject, not just with the American market; figures of Washington, Lincoln and Jefferson were also produced.

▶ **"Cnl Simpson"**
Sir James Simpson (1792–1868) was second-in-command to Sir Charles Napier during the Kacchi expedition in 1845, and was later Chief-of-Staff during the Crimean War of 1854–56, before succeeding to Commander of the British troops after the death of Lord Raglan in 1855. He received a knighthood for his services during the Crimean War and his capture of the Russian fort Sebastopol. Crimean War figures are worth buying if reasonably priced, as this is a very popular area. This figure pairs with Sir George Brown.

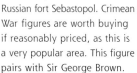

"Cnl Simpson", c.1854, ht 33cm/13in, **£600–700/ $950–1,100**

"The Sultan"

Abd-ul-Medjid (1823–61) succeeded his father as Sultan of Turkey in 1839, and played an active part as an ally of England and France during the Crimean War. Many figures of Medjid were produced as he was popular in the West. Group figures were produced of him with Victoria and Napoleon III, called "Turkey–England–France". There is also a standing figure entitled "Sultan", sourced from an engraving in The Illustrated London News. This figure is in a "series", i.e. one of 4 or 6 different figures. It pairs with either Marshal Arnaud or Omar Pasha; the other figure in the set is Lord Raglan, who faces the same way as the Sultan (all were commanders in the Crimean War).

"The Sultan", c.1854,
ht 28cm/11in,
**£450–550/
$725–875**

"G. Brown", c.1854, ht 33cm/13in,
£600–700/$950–1,100

▲ "G. Brown"

Sir George Brown (1790–1865) distinguished himself during the Peninsular War of 1812–13, earning a knighthood for his services, and later commanded the Light Division during the Crimean War of 1854–56. Many figures such as this were made in pairs, which are more valuable, so it is worth buying a single in the hope of finding its pair. This figure pairs with Sir James Simpson, another Crimean War veteran.

FACT FILE

Spotting quality figures

All Staffordshire figures are hand-painted, and figures decorated with underglaze blue and full enamel colours are the most collectable. The better modelled and sharper the features, the earlier the figure was made from the mould: these early pieces are the most expensive and highly sought after.

▼ "Eliza Cook"

Eliza Cook (1818–89) was the daughter of a London tradesman. She wrote and published poems, which were collected in the The Eliza Cook Journals. Although popular at the time, Eliza Cook is now almost completely forgotten. This is an "Alpha Factory" figure – the indented titling seen here is one of their hallmarks. "Alpha Factory" is the name given to a particular style of figure, and it is possible that a factory of this name never existed. The figures could have been the work of a particular modeller who worked for a number of potteries. Such figures are always well modelled and decorated.

"Eliza Cook",
c.1850, ht
27.5cm/10¾in,
**£250–350/
$400–550**

"Sir Walter Scott", c.1850,
ht 27.5cm/10¾in, **£400–500/
$650–800**

"Death of Nelson",
c.1850, ht 20.5cm/8in,
£300–500/$475–800

"W. Codrington", c.1854,
ht 34.5cm/13½in,
£1,000–2,000/$1,600–3,200

▲ "W. Codrington"

Sir William John Codrington
(1804–84) was Commander of
the Light Division during the
Crimean War, and Commander-
in-Chief of the Crimean forces.
He later went into politics,
and from 1859–65 was the
Governor-General of Gibraltar.
As well as standing figures of
Codrington, figures of him on
horseback were produced that
pair with General Pellissier, the
Commander-in-Chief of the
French forces in the Crimea.
This figure can also be found
untitled, though the majority
of military figures are titled.

▲ "Sir Walter Scott"

Born in Edinburgh, Sir Walter
Scott (1771–1832) was called
to the bar in 1792, and in
1814 published his first novel,
Waverley. For the next six years
he published a new novel every
year, all the time keeping his
identity secret, as he felt that
the writing of novels was below
the dignity of an eminent
lawyer. It may be noted that
only two figures of Scott were
produced and both of them
pair with Robert Burns. This
particular figure is recorded in
three sizes, 24cm/9½in, 27.5cm/
10¾in (as here) and 37cm/
14½in, the two larger versions
pairing with Robert Burns.

▲ "Death of Nelson"

Lord Horatio Nelson (1758–
1805) was born in Norfolk
and became probably the
most famous English seaman
in history. He was appointed
Commander-in-Chief of the
Mediterranean in 1803, making
the *Victory* his flagship. His
orders were to encounter the
French fleet, which he did at
Cape Trafalgar in the famous
Battle of Trafalgar. The English
victory complete, Nelson was
shot on his quarter-deck from
the *Redoubtable* on the way
back home and died within
the hour. This was a popular
subject for the potters, with
many versions being made.

Checking condition
When inspecting a figure, look at the exposed parts first for damage, such as the neck of the figure, the hands, and any other parts that have been made from separate moulds. Good condition is essential, as worn or heavily crazed figures with flaking enamels will be reduced in value.

"Sir Robert Peel", c.1845, ht 21cm/ 8¼in, **£500–600/$800–950**

▲ Two figures of "Sir Robert Peel"

Sir Robert Peel (1788–1850) founded the Metropolitan Police Force in 1829, and was British Prime Minister from 1834–35. He opposed the Repeal of the Corn Laws in 1845, and a few months later was defeated on the Irish Bill and retired from office. In 1850 he was thrown from his horse on Constitutional Hill in London and died three days later from his injuries. He was a very popular politician of the time, and over 16 different models were made of him in various poses – standing, seated and on horseback. The two figures illustrated here appear identical but there are slight modelling differences.

"Jemmy Wood", c.1840, ht 19cm/7½in, **£250–350/ $400–550**

▲ "Jemmy Wood"

Jemmy Wood (1756–1836) was a wealthy draper from Westgate, Gloucester. On his death he left £781,000/$1,250,000, divided between four executors. However, a codicil sent anonymously to a Mr Helps left £200,000/ $320,000 to Gloucester city, with Mr Helps also benefiting. The Council took legal action against Helps but lost the case. An obscure subject for the potters to choose, it shows the public interest in the case, as this is one of three different models.

Maria Manning, c.1849, ht 24cm/ 9½in, **£900–1,100/$1,450–1,750**

▲ Maria Manning

Maria Manning (1821–49), with her husband Frederick, murdered Patrick O'Connor at their home in Bermondsey, London. Found guilty, they were both hanged. Often figures were made of the houses where the crimes were committed, but no figure of 3 Milniver Place has ever been recorded. This figure pairs with Frederick Manning.

▼ "Sir R Tichbourne"

This commemorates a celebrated trial of the Victorian era. Lowly butcher, Arthur Orton, returned from Australia posing as Sir Roger Tichbourne, 10th Baronet, to claim his estate. Although "recognized" as her eldest son by Lady Tichbourne, Orton was charged with perjury and sent to prison for 14 years. Released in 1884, he became a famous theatre act; these figures would have been sold at his shows.

"Sir R Tichbourne", c.1880, ht 37.5cm/14¾in, **£350–450/ $550–725**

▼ "John Brown"

John Brown (1800–59) was an active abolitionist of the slave trade, and he established a refuge for runaway slaves in the United States. In 1859 he led a raid on the US armoury at Harpers Ferry, West Virginia, where he took hostages. Colonel Robert E. Lee arrived with a platoon of marines and retook the armoury. Brown was badly wounded and was sentenced to hanging. This is a rare figure which is avidly sought after by American collectors. A version is also recorded at 34.5cm/13½in.

"John Brown", c.1860, ht 28cm/ 11in, **£400–600/$650–950**

▼ "D O'Connell"

Daniel O'Connell (1775–1847) was elected Member of Parliament for Clare in Ireland in 1828. He could not take his seat because he was a Catholic, but he was re-elected after the Catholic Emancipation Act of 1830, before being imprisoned in 1844 for sedition. He died on his way from Ireland to Rome. O'Connell was a popular politician of his time. This figure never had a pair, but more than 5 different versions of him were made, with many exported to the Irish market.

"D O'Connell", c.1850, ht 35.5cm/ 14in, **£700–900/$1,125–1,450**

"Moody"

Born in Massachusetts, Dwight Lyman Moody (1837–99) opened a Sunday school in Chicago in 1858, which later became the Chicago Avenue Church. With his friend Ira David Sankey he toured England in 1873, 1881 and 1882. This figure, titled in raised gilt capitals, pairs with Ira David Sankey with whom he co-wrote *Sacred Songs and Solos*, a book of music that sold over 500,000 copies. The figure of Moody can be found in four different sizes, 25cm/9¾in, 29cm/11½in, 34.5cm/13½in (illustrated here) and 43.5cm/17in.

"Moody", c.1871, ht 34.5cm/13½in, **£300–400/$475–650**

"James B Rush" and "Emily Sandford"

James Bloomfield Rush, tenant of Potash Farm near Wymondham in Norfolk was charged with the murder of his landlord Isaac Jermy and Jermy's son-in-law at Stanfield Hall in 1849. He was convicted largely on the evidence of his mistress, Emily Sandford, and hanged and buried at Norwich Castle. Figures of Stanfield Hall, Potash Farm and Norwich Castle were also made, reflecting the Victorian fascination with grisly murders.

"James B Rush" & "Emily Sandford", c. 1849, ht 26.5cm/10½in, **£1,600–1,800/$2,600–2,900**

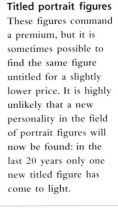

Titled portrait figures

These figures command a premium, but it is sometimes possible to find the same figure untitled for a slightly lower price. It is highly unlikely that a new personality in the field of portrait figures will now be found: in the last 20 years only one new titled figure has come to light.

"T S Duncombe"

Thomas Slingsby Duncombe (1796–1861) was a Member of Parliament from 1826–61 and President of Trade. In 1848, he delivered to the House of Commons the People's Petition, which had over three million signatories. He is probably most remembered as one of the best-dressed men in the House of Commons. This rare piece – the only recorded version of this figure – is highly sought after by collectors.

"T S Duncombe", c.1845, ht 23cm/9in, **£1,000–2,000/ $1,600–3,200**

Naval & military figures

The Victorian era saw a constant series of international battles and conflicts in which the British played a major role. The potters produced portrait figures of the generals, colonels and admirals who led the various armies and navies, appealing to the patriotic nature of the British public, and found an even greater market for the sentimental subjects of soldiers and sailors leaving or returning to their loved ones. The Crimean War of 1854–56 produced a rush of commemorative figures and the majority of military and naval figures apply to this conflict. Having established a market, subsequent battles (the Indian Mutiny of 1857, the Franco-Prussian War of 1870 and the Boer War of 1901) prompted further production but the quality of these was not as good.

▶ **Pair of sailors standing beside barrels**
These types of figures are never found with particularly good colouring. They were mostly produced in the 1860s, so it is therefore more than possible that they are not attributed to a particular war or conflict, but rather that the potters, knowing that sailors were still a popular subject with the public, carried on pro-ducing them for this reason alone. In view of the attire of the man on the left, it is possible that these figures are of theatrical inspiration. Figures of this kind are quite commonly found and the lower price range reflects this.

Pair of sailors standing beside barrels, c.1860, ht 30.5cm/12in, **£250–300/ $400–475**

▼ **"The Sailor's Return"**
Many figures such as this were produced, celebrating a sailor's safe return from the wars, back into the arms of his wife or sweetheart. Not all figures were titled, and it is possible that many of the figures produced could in fact have represented the sailor going off to war. However, no figure has ever been found entitled "Sailor's Farewell", although there are various figures depicting a soldier and his girl, most of which are given the title "Soldier's Farewell".

"The Sailor's Return", c.1855, ht 30.5cm/12in, **£400–500/$650–800**

FACT FILE

Pricing of naval and military figures
Untitled figures of this type were produced in their thousands and in varying degrees of quality. Overshadowed by portrait figures for many years, they can often still be a reasonable price and prove a good investment.

▼ "The Wounded Soldier"

This type of figure proved very popular in Britain in the mid-19thC and would have been placed with pride on mantelpieces across the country. Such pride is also reflected in the potters' work in this particular figure, as all versions of it are always well coloured. Its source and inspiration was an engraving published in *Cassell's Illustrated Family Paper* on 7 April 1855, entitled "Landing of the Invalided". This figure can also be found at 23cm/9in.

"The Wounded Soldier", c.1855, ht 33cm/13in, **£500–600/ $800–950**

Pair of Prussian generals on horseback, c.1870, ht 32cm/12½in, **£600–700/$950–1,100**

▲ Pair of Prussian generals

This pair dates from the Franco-Prussian War of 1870 and shows that, even though the general quality of Staffordshire figures was in decline, potters were still able to produce fine figures at this date. The use of underglaze blue was all but discontinued by this time, but the potters have still produced a well-coloured and well-modelled figure. Another pair, produced to commemorate this conflict, is almost identical to this one, except that the soldiers wear plumed hats and the position of their arms is slightly different.

▼ "The Soldier's Return"

Similar to "The Sailor's Return" and produced around the same time, this figure is classed as quite rare as it is not so easily found. Unlike the sailor figure, it does have a counterpart, which although not a true pair is titled "The Soldier's Farewell", and is sourced from a Baxter print. There is one other known titled piece and other untitled representations of this theme.

"The Soldier's Return", c.1855, ht 30.5cm/12in, **£600–700/ $950–1,100**

Sporting figures

With the widespread media coverage that sport commands today, it is easy to forget that in the Victorian era sport was only accessible through attending the event. Relatively few figures associated with sport were made, which perhaps reflects this limited access. Many team games were still in their infancy – the only example of a football figure is a late figure of a boy with a football and there are no figures relating to rugby or golf. Of the rare figures of sport that the potters did make, figures of cricketers, boxers and jockeys seemed to prevail. Today, any figure with a sporting connection will command a high price. Care should be taken, as there are many reproductions of sporting figures on the market, most notably of cricketers and boxers.

▼ Pair of cricketers
This fine pair always commands a high price, appealing not only to collectors of cricket memorabilia but to all kinds of collectors. The identity of these two men has never been confirmed as they are always found untitled. Other versions of cricketers include a similar pair at 26.5cm/10½in, although care should be taken as there are many reproductions of this version, and a set of three spill vases of the cricketers Box, Clark and Fuller Pitch.

Pair of cricketers, c.1855, ht 35.5cm/14in, **£3,000–4,000/ $4,800–6,400**

▲ Boys playing cricket
A rare pair of figures, care should be taken when buying these as reproductions of them have been made since about 1985, believed to be from the Isle of Man. The reproductions are made from the slip-mould method, so when handling they feel lighter than their Victorian counterparts. They are also normally brightly painted, and have a heavy, fake "craquelure".

Pair of figures of boys playing cricket, c.1855, ht 17cm/6¾in, **£1,500–2,000/ $2,400–3,200**

Pair of jockeys, c.1860, ht 23cm/9in, **£700–900/ $1,100–1,450**

Reproductions & fakes

Early reproductions of these figures came from the Isle of Wight and more recently have been made in the Far East using the press-mould method. Many are deliberate fakes as no makers' marks are put on the bases, or these marks are subsequently removed. A fake is worth £150/$240.

FACT FILE

▼ "Heenan–Sayers"

John Carmel Heenan (1835–73), a heavyweight bare-knuckle fighter from New York State, and Tom Sayers (1826–65), English middleweight champion from 1857, met in April 1865 at Farnborough; the result was a draw. This figure can also be found at 23cm/9in but there is another very rare version, which is almost identical apart from being 34.5cm/13½in high and titled "Sayers & Heenan" in gilt.

"Heenan–Sayers", c.1860, ht 25.5cm/ 10in, **£600–700/$950–1,100**

▲ Pair of jockeys

Six different versions of jockeys have been recorded but they are still very rare and difficult to come by. The figures are normally decorated in the way illustrated above, with the area below the horse left white and the jacket of the jockey rarely in underglaze blue, although it has been found coloured on the odd occasion. These figures may also be found at 15cm/6in.

▼ Galloping jockeys

This is a particularly rare pair dating from c.1870. They are unusual as the decorators have gone to considerable trouble in painting the horses, with detailed brushstrokes on the body and base, but the jockeys have hardly any colouring at all. This is the only version to portray the horses galloping.

Pair of jockeys on galloping horses, c.1870, ht 18.5cm/ 7¼in, **£1,300–1,500/ $2,100–2,400**

Religious figures

Religion and the temperance movement, which forbade the consumption of alcohol, were important features of Victorian life. Religion was at its height and churches of many denominations were full; the rise of Methodism, begun by John Wesley during the 18thC, was still a driving force. The potters responded by producing religious figures from the Old and New Testaments, including the gospel writers Matthew, Mark, Luke and John. Figures of preachers such as John Wesley, John Brown, Adam Clarke, Christmas Evans and Charles Spurgeon were modelled, as were members of the temperance movement, including the Band of Hope and the Independent Order of the Good Templars. Figures of holy water stoups (*see* p.59) were also produced, depicting Christ on the cross with a well for the water below.

▶ **Figure of Christ**
This figure is known as "The Flagellation" and is similar in appearance to a bronze sculpture from Louis XIV's collection at the Louvre Museum in Paris. Christ was a popular figure to be modelled by the potters, and many different versions were produced: not only figures of him alone, but also group figures (such as with the "Woman of Sameria"), titled figures such as "Christ Restoring the Sight to the Blind", and figures showing children at his side entitled "Forbid Them Not". This figure here may also be found at 42.5cm/16¾in.

Figure of Christ, c.1855,
ht 38cm/15in,
£300–400/$475–650

▼ **Figure of Rebekah and Abraham's servant**
The inspiration for this popular piece comes from a painting by the famous French painter Horace Vernet, which was engraved by J. Rogers for a print in an illuminated Bible called *Family Devotions*. Many versions of this figure were made; most notable were those that had a water well instead of a spill opening. This figure comes in three sizes.

Rebekah & Abraham's servant, c.1855,
ht 25.5cm/10in,
£250–350/ $400–550

▼ Figure of Mary with the infant Jesus

A number of Staffordshire figures of Mary and the infant Jesus were produced, as were figures depicting Joseph with Jesus. Group figures of Mary, Joseph and the infant Jesus were also potted, and entitled "Flight to Egypt". It should be noted that religious figures are normally sparsely coloured, and it is rare to find versions in full colour. Underglaze blue, in particular, is known to have been used on only a handful of models depicting religious themes.

Mary and the infant Jesus, c.1860, ht 32cm/12½in, **£200–300/ $325–475**

Figure of Balaam and his ass, c.1860, ht 26.5cm/10½in, **£300–400/$475–650**

▲ Balaam and his ass

Although it is not titled, this figure is known to represent Balaam and his ass, taken from the Old Testament, Chapter 22, Verse 23. The potters produced many biblical figures, including Moses, Daniel, Ruth, Samson, Saul, Samuel and Lot and his daughters.

Price of religious figures

Other than portrait figures of specific contemporary religious people, these figures have not been well catalogued until comparatively recently. Partly for that reason, they are still the least expensive of all the categories, with the exception of miniatures.

▼ "Fountain 1861"

This figure was produced to commemorate the opening of pure water fountains across the country in the 1860s. Until this time, it was thought safer to drink beer than water. These fountains were installed by local philanthropists or members of the temperance movement. The facial features of the man and one of the women bear a striking familiarity to that of Prince Louis of Hesse and Princess Alice. It may be that they were patrons of the "fountains", though there is no evidence to prove this.

"Fountain 1861", c.1861, ht 39.5cm/ 15½in, **£300–400/ $475–650**

Houses, castles & churches

Figures of houses, castles and churches were initially made as pastille burners. A pastille (a small tablet that, when lit, gave off a pleasant scent) was placed in the receptacle in the back of the figure and its scented smoke would escape via the chimney, tower or turret. They were, in effect, incense burners, and were used to overpower the more unpleasant smells that were common in the majority of towns and cities, which had limited sanitary conditions in an era before proper sewerage or drainage. As conditions improved, there was less need for pastille burners and the potters converted many of them to decorative objects or even money-boxes. Having established a market for these new ornaments, many more were made, including some weird and wonderful pieces.

▼ **Castle with a clockface**
This figure is the creation of a potter's vivid imagination. It is highly unlikely that a castle of this construction ever existed and the leaves of the grapevine are clearly out of proportion with the building, but these quirks simply add to the charm of the piece. The clockface shows nine o'clock: there is no known significance to the times shown on these clockfaces, although the hands are usually positioned vertically, showing either 12.30 or six o'clock.

Castle with a clockface, c.1860, ht 25.5cm/10in, **£240–280/ $375–450**

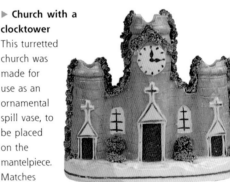

▶ **Church with a clocktower**
This turretted church was made for use as an ornamental spill vase, to be placed on the mantelpiece. Matches were expensive at the time; instead pieces of newspaper were rolled into thin spills, and then a light obtained from the fire to light the master's pipe, a candle, or perhaps a gas mantle in wealthier homes. This particular figure has bricklike indentations on both the front and back, although the back is otherwise undecorated.

Church with a clocktower, c.1850, ht 16.5cm/6½in, **£100–150/ $160–250**

"Stanfield Hall" & "Potash Farm", c.1849, ht 14cm/5½in, **£250–350/ $400–550** (each)

▲ "Stanfield Hall" and "Potash Farm"

These two figures have been transposed, as each has the other's title. The tenant of Potash Farm, James Bloomfield Rush, murdered his landlord, Isaac Jermy, and Jermy's son-in-law, at their home, Stanfield Hall, in 1849. This was a celebrated murder case, with Rush's mistress Emily Sandford giving evidence against him. Figures of Sandford and Rush can be found (see p.43), as well as a very rare figure of Norwich Castle, where Rush was hanged. This pair was also made at 21.5cm/8½in.

▼ "Windsor Lodge"

Within the series of titled castles (see Fact File), there are a number with royal connections, such as "Balmoral Castle", of which two versions are known, and "Caernarvon Castle". There is also a figure recorded of "Windsor Castle". The particular figure illustrated here, of Windsor Lodge, is something of an anomaly, as although there is a Royal Lodge and a Queen's Lodge at Windsor, there is no Windsor Lodge, and no trace of a cottage resembling this figure has ever been recorded at or near Windsor Castle.

"Windsor Lodge", c.1855, ht 15cm/ 6in, **£350–450/ $550–725**

▼ Figure of a castle
This figure is a triple pastille burner. A surprising number of cottages, castles and other pastille burners are decorated in this salmon colour, presumably because it imitated the colour of brickwork. However, the most sought-after and expensive of the pastille burners are the lilac-coloured figures: often prices in excess of £1,000/ $1,600 can be paid for these. Later versions of this figure, converted from the original pastille burners, can be found with the doorways and windows filled in.

Figure of a castle, c.1860, ht 19cm/ 7½in, **£150–250/$250–400**

Miniature figures

Many people have dismissed all Victorian Staffordshire figures as cheap "fairings", which were small pieces of pottery or porcelain commonly given away at fair stalls as prizes. This is patently not the case: the vast majority of the figures made would have been far too expensive at the time to have been simply given away. However, miniatures, do fall into the category of fairings, as these were produced in enormous quantities. Contemporary records show that one small boy working for a potter could have made about 140,000 figures in a year. This rate of production, coupled with the paltry wages paid to such children, would have made the figures such a price that the fairs could afford to buy them and then give them away.

Man, c.1860, ht 4.5cm/1¾in, £75–85/ $125–140

▼ Pair of seated spaniels and a standing poodle

Pair of spaniels, c.1855, ht 7.5cm/3in, £100–150/ $160–250 (the pair); poodle, c.1855, ht 4.5cm/1¾in, £40–60/ $65–95

The maximum size for a miniature can be considered to be 10–11.5cm/4–4½in; most miniatures are 5–9cm/ 2–3½in. The pair of spaniels illustrated below are parti-cularly well modelled and decorated for their size, and represent, as a pair, among the most expensive miniatures available. The single poodle, as with larger versions of any figure, would be purchased at approximately one-third of the price of a pair.

▶ Man and pairs of dogs

Miniatures need to be displayed in quantity, as shown here, for their charm to be appreciated. The man could be a miniature version of Robert Trogwy Evans, a Welsh religious minister, or of the murderer, William Palmer. It is difficult to tell at this size, and miniatures are rarely titled. Of the two pairs of dogs, the seated pair are more expensive.

Dogs, c.1855, ht 7.5cm/3in, £80–100/ $130–160 (each pair)

Girl with rabbits, John Wesley and arbour group of two lovers, all c.1855, hts 6.5–7.5cm/2½–3in, **£30–40/$50–65**

Purpose of miniatures

An alternative theory states that miniature figures were made as travelling salesmen's samples, as a number of figures do exist in both small and large sizes. However, the majority do not, and it is highly unlikely, therefore, that this theory is accurate. More likely is that they were inexpensive ornaments used as fairings.

FACT FILE

Spill vase girl, Little Red Riding Hood and money-box heads, all c.1855, hts 4–7.5cm/1½–3in, **£30–40/ $50–65**; Napoleon, c.1855, ht 8cm/3¼in, **£60–70/$95–110**

▲ Young girl, John Wesley and arbour group of lovers

The figure of the girl with two rabbits and a hutch would have had a pair, most likely a mirror image with a boy replacing the girl. There are no large versions known of these figures, or the arbour figure of the two lovers. Potters made savings on miniature figures as they rarely used underglaze blue enamels and gilding in their decoration. The figure of John Wesley can be found in many sizes and variations, ranging from 7.5–20.5cm/3–8in. He died in 1791 but his ideas remained very popular, forming the basis of the Methodist movement.

▶ Spill vase girl, Napoleon Bonaparte, Little Red Riding Hood and money-box heads

The figures of Napoleon and Little Red Riding Hood are unusual as they are smaller versions of large figures (61cm/24in and 38cm/15in respectively). The spill-vase figure of the girl would have had a pair, a mirror image with the girl replaced by a boy. The heads are difficult to find as they were given to children to store money and as the only opening was the slot at the top, most heads were smashed in order to get the money out.

Late figures

The Victorian era ended in 1901 with the death of Victoria and the ascension of Edward VII, and by this time Staffordshire figure production was in decline. Underglaze blue, the hallmark of the mid-19th century, was no longer used and most figures had little or no decoration. If they were gilded at all it was not with soft "best gold" but with harsh "bright gold" that was painted on after glazing and did not need burnishing. A few new figures were made but the majority were from old moulds of diminishing quality. The Kent factory (who acquired moulds from the Parr factory and other defunct potteries) and the Sampson Smith factory produced most of the late 19th and early 20thC figures: mainly white or underglaze brown dogs and lions, some with glass eyes.

Figure of King Henry V, c.1880, ht 38cm/15in, **£200–300/$325–475**

▶ **King Henry V**
This is one of few new later theatrical figures. It was probably copied from a Parian figure – a type of white pottery that was popular in the Victorian era and produced by Minton, among others. It bears many of the hallmarks of a later piece, being sparsely decorated and using "bright gold" gilding. It has never been recorded as fully coloured or with underglaze blue. It is known to be by the Sampson Smith factory as it is illustrated in one of their catalogues.

▼ **"G. Gordon"**
General Gordon was killed at the siege of Khartoum in 1885, which had lasted for over 300 days. The figure illustrated was made at about this time, and was probably a memorial to the general. This particular example is sparsely coloured but, unusually for such a late figure, can also be found with an underglaze blue or red overglaze tunic. A number of versions of Gordon were made, including a titled figure of him seated on a camel, sourced from a sculpture by Onslow Ford R.A., now on display at Gillingham's School of Military Engineering, Kent.

"G. Gordon", c.1885, ht 44.5cm/17½in, **£300–350/$475–550**

20thC figures

The production of Staffordshire figures ceased in 1962 with the closure of the Kent factory. It is difficult to distinguish the exact date of figures made between 1900 and 1962, and many 20thC figures are simply sold as being "c.1900" in origin.

FACT FILE

▼ Edward VII and Alexandra

Figures of the new King and Queen were the last royal pieces produced by the potteries. This pair, made by the Kent factory, are an imposing size but the quality of modelling and decoration has declined. Other potters made versions of them standing, and on horses.

King Edward VII and Queen Alexandra, c.1901, ht 35.5cm/14in, **£300–350/$475–550**

Pair of seated giraffes, c.1890, ht 16.5cm/6½in, **£700–800/$1,100–1,300**

▲ Pair of seated giraffes

Even though these are late figures, their subject matter makes them very sought after. They are copies of earlier pieces that would have been made c.1860 by the Parr factory. These figures were made by the Kent factory and while they are well modelled and coloured, when placed along-side an earlier example, the difference in quality is clear. The earlier models command at least double the price.

▼ Lion with its paw on a ball

After 1885 there was a change in the decoration of animal figures: rather than painting in the eyes of the dogs and lions, the potters started to use glass eyes instead, mostly on the larger figures, as here. This has now become a good guide to dating these later figures. Other figures of lions were produced at this time, the most notable with glass eyes, standing four square without a base. Although the modelling and colouring of this figure is poor, it does possess a naive charm.

Lion and ball, c.1900, ht 28cm/11in, **£120–140/$200–225**

Reproductions & fakes

There are reproductions of many diverse figures in the marketplace and the new collector should be a little wary. During the 1970s and '80s, they were produced by the slip-mould method, making them much lighter than their Victorian counterparts. However, since the 1990s the press–mould method has been used (for example in the Far East), making the new figures a similar weight to the originals and therefore difficult to identify. An experienced eye can spot a reproduction immediately, but for those starting out it is harder to find the tell-tale signs, such as poorly applied colour and gilding; it is only through handling the originals and comparing the two together over a period of time that the differences will become apparent. If a piece seems to be priced too reasonably, and you are not sure, it is always best to side with caution. The distinction between reproductions and fakes is that reproductions are later versions of old models, whereas fakes are deliberate deceptions, of which there are few at this moment.

"The Minstrel", c.1985, ht 25.5cm/10in, **£15/$25**

▼ **"The Minstrel"**
This is a copy of a genuine figure, produced by the slip-mould method with a fake title applied to make it seem more valuable. On this occasion, to deceive further, a fake craquelure has been effected. The glaze, essentially a very thin sheet of glass, sometimes cracks or crazes on genuine figures as the clay shrinks underneath. This effect can be replicated and is therefore not always a sign of age. The colours used on this figure are not the same as on a genuine Staffordshire figure. The glaze is also too thin and even to be original.

▶ **"Fred Archer"**
This figure was also produced by the slip-mould method, where a mould was taken from a genuine figure. Such reproductions are produced in pairs; a genuine pair would cost in excess of £1,000/$1,600. The originals were untitled, and this fake title is of a style that did not appear on genuine figures. Fred Archer was a real jockey but no contemporary figures of him were made.

"Fred Archer", c.1985, ht 30.5cm/12in, **£25/$40**

Figure of a sleeping soldier,
c.1998, ht 28cm/11in, **£25/$40**

▲ **Figure of a sleeping soldier**
This figure has been imported
from the Far East and has
been made by the press-mould
method, as the original figure
would have been. From the
photograph above it is very
difficult to tell that this figure
is a reproduction: the colouring
is quite authentic, in particular
the underglaze blue. This
figure is a direct copy of the
original and there are a number
of different versions to be
found, one of which is entitled
"Soldier's Dream". This is the
perfect example of a very good
imitation reproduction that will
often be passed off as genuine.

Spaniel with basket, c.1860,
ht 26.5cm/10½in, **£70/$110**

▲ **Spaniel with basket**
This is a genuine Staffordshire
figure of a seated spaniel.
However, it is classified as a
fake because the basket has
been added on quite recently.
This has been done entirely
for commercial reasons: a pair
of black and white dogs
without a basket in their
mouths would be worth
c.£300–400/$475–650.
With the addition of
a basket, had they
been genuine,
they would retail
for around
£1,200–1,500/
$1,925–2,400
for the pair.

Spotting a fake
Care should be taken
when looking for
authenticity, as inten-
tional damage has been
seen made to repro-
ductions, in the hope of
convincing the potential
buyer that it is a damaged
but genuine example.
With the escalating
prices of Staffordshire,
other ingenious fakes are
likely to appear so be
vigilant when buying.

▼ **Pair of spaniels**
This figure, and its pair lying
down, are produced by the
slip-mould method. The gold,
unlike on earlier figures, has
been applied by painting, and
no further firing would have
been necessary. Quite often
with new slip-mould figures,
the hole on the bottom of the
figure is substantially larger
than on earlier figures. Also the
base on these reproductions is
completely flat and unglazed,
as opposed to the concave
and glazed bases of genuine
figures (see base on p.7).

Pair of spaniels,
c.1970, ht
13cm/5in,
£30/$50

Other uses

As we have seen, not all Staffordshire figures were produced just for decorative purposes. The potters also produced figures and items with a specific use, some of which have already been mentioned. Some of the many functional items produced for this mass market are shown below.

Candlestick holders were quite rare, which is surprising considering that the majority of homes relied on this type of light. These figures came in a variety of forms, normally in pairs.

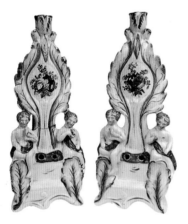

▲ Watch-holder figure of a girl and a boy standing cross-legged either side of a vine, one hand on their hip and the other holding a bird, c.1855, ht 26.5cm/10½in, **£200–£250/$325–400**

▲ Two figures of candlestick holders (with holes for holding pens), c.1865, ht 25cm/10in, **£60–80/$95–125** (each)

Spill vases, or holders, held the twisted sheets of paper (spills) that supplemented matches and proper tapers, which were too expensive for the average Victorian household's income.

Watch holders were used to display pocket watches. Watches and clocks were an expensive luxury and usually only the man of the house had a timepiece. When he returned from a day's work, he would place his pocket watch in the watch holder for the family to use as a clock.

▲ Watch-holder figure of a girl and boy, c.1850, ht 30.5cm/12in, **£200–250/$325–400**

Holy water stoups, small receptacles, were probably copied and adapted by the potters from those in use in Roman Catholic churches, and supplied to people for use in their homes. The figures normally take the form of Mary and the baby Jesus, either on their own or accompanied by angels standing beside them, with the stoup below to hold the holy water.

Creamers (jugs for cream) took a number of forms, the most recognizable being the figure of a cow, with its open mouth forming the spout, its tail or a milkmaid or man modelled as the handle, and a hole on its back for the milk or cream to be poured into. Most of these figures started life with a small cover for the hole, but the majority of covers are now missing. Creamers were made both prior to and throughout the Victorian period.

Money boxes are normally found in the shape of houses, but some were made as caricature heads (see p.53). However, they are a rarity as many were broken to retrieve the money inside, (though the money can be extracted with a knife).

Sanders were used to sprinkle fine sand on to wet ink to stop it from smudging. Blotting paper was not as prevalent as it is today so this method was more commonly used. These sanders normally took the form of a man, with holes in the top of his hat providing the sprinkler.

Pastille burners were used in domestic homes to try and alleviate the terrible problem of sanitary conditions in towns and cities. Pastilles were tablets that gave off a scent when lit and these were placed in the burners to mask any unpleasant smells. The pastille burners came in many shapes and sizes, principally houses, churches and castles, and had an opening in the back in which to place the pastille. The chimney, tower, or turret on the top of the building would allow the smoke to escape.

Pen or quill holders came in many forms, and can normally be identified very quickly by the hole for the pen. Many examples were produced, one of the most common being seated whippets with the hole in front of them, which sometimes even had a gilt ring around it.

▲ Two pen/quill holders in the form of men's heads, c.1835, ht 5cm/2in, **£120–150/$200–250** (per head)

Tobacco (snuff) jars normally come in the form of a seated man or woman, or occasionally just a head, with a hat forming the lid of the jar. A few trinket boxes were made in a similar fashion, though these were usually in the form of a woman and came apart at the waist instead.

▼ Tobacco jar, woman with head and shoulders forming the lid, c.1870, ht 30.5cm/12in, **£250–300/$400–475**

Glossary

Best gold An early form of gilding, which required burnishing after firing

Biscuit Unglazed porcelain or earthenware fired once only. The term also refers to white porcelain (especially figures) that has been left unglazed and undecorated)

Bocage Densely-encrusted flowering tree stumps supporting a group or as a backdrop

Body The material from which pottery is made. Also refers to the main part of a piece

Bright gold A late form of gilding that superseded best gold and was less expensive and quicker to apply, but which gave a brassy rather than a gold finish

Cobalt blue A colour, discovered in 1830 that could be applied to figures prior to glazing; a hallmark of figures made between 1840 and 1865

Comforters The name given to the pairs of spaniel figures that sat either side of a mantelpiece, known in Scotland as "Wally Dogs"

Craquelure Cracks in the glaze caused naturally by the shrinking of the pottery over time; this can be replicated artificially

Craze Tiny, undesirable surface cracks caused by shrinking in the glaze, or other technical defects

Documentary piece Wares that bear evidence indicating their origin, such as the signature of the decorator or modeller

Fairings Inexpensive figures, sometimes miniatures, produced in bulk for the purpose of becoming prizes given away at fairs; usually have little or no decoration

Feathering The application of paint using hundreds of short, layered brushstrokes to build up colour and definition; used on earlier Staffordshire figures

Fire cracks The term for the splitting in the body that can appear after firing. Usually regarded as acceptable damage

Firing The process of baking ceramics in a kiln. Temperatures range from 800°C (142°F) for earthenware to 1,450°C (2,642°F) for some hard-paste porcelain and stoneware

Flatbacks Staffordshire figures and groups made from about 1840 until early in the 20thC. As the name implies, the backs are almost flat and undecorated as they were principally intended for the mantelpiece.

Gilding The application of gold paint to decorate a figure

Glaze A glassy coating painted, dusted or sprayed onto the surface of porcelain; becomes smooth and shiny after firing, making the body non-porous

Glost oven A very high-temperature oven used for hardening the glaze

Ground The background or base colour, to which decoration and gilding are applied

Impressed Indented marks and hallmarks, as opposed to incised

Incised Scratched into the surface of a piece.

"In the white" Undecorated porcelain wares

Kiln Oven used for the setting of the transfer before glazing

Lustre The application of metallic oxide, which gave a purple or copper colour and was applied instead of enamel or underglaze colours

Overglaze Decoration painted in enamels or transfer-printed on top of a fired glaze

Pratt ware Early 19thC creamware decorated in high-fired colours such as ochre, yellow, green, brown and blue.

Press-moulding The moulding of figures achieved by pressing clay into an absorbent mould

Rococo A type of base that incorporates a scroll motif, either in shape or in decoration

Slip Smooth dilution of clay and water used in the making and decoration of pottery

Slip-moulding The moulding of figures by pouring slip, which is clay with the consistency of cream, into a pre-formed hollow mould

Spill vase A figure with an opening at the top to hold strips of wood, paper etc to light pipes from the fire

Underglaze The application of colour to a biscuit figure prior to its firing

What to read

Halfpenny, Pat
*English Earthenware Figures
1740-1840*
(Antique Collectors Club, 1991)

Harding, Adrian & Nicholas
*Victorian Staffordshire Figures
1835-1875 Book One*
(Schiffer Publishing, USA, 1998)

Harding, Adrian & Nicholas
*Victorian Staffordshire Figures
1835-1875 Book Two*
(Schiffer Publishing, USA, 1998)

Harding, Adrian & Nicholas
*Victorian Staffordshire Figures
1835-1875 The Addendum*
(Schiffer Publishing, USA, 2000)

Hodkinson, Malcolm & Judith
*Sherratt: A Natural Family
of Staffordshire Figures*
(Chisquare, USA, 1991)

Oliver, Anthony
*Staffordshire Pottery:
The Tribal Art of England*
(Heinemann, London, 1981)

Oliver, Anthony
The Victorian Staffordshire Figure
(Heinemann, London, 1971)

Pope, Clive Mason
A-Z of Staffordshire Dogs
(Private Publication, 1990;
new edition Antique Collectors
Club, 1998)

Pugh, P.D. Gordon
Staffordshire Portrait Figures
(Barrie & Jenkins,
London, 1970)

Where to see and buy

The best place to see and handle genuine Staffordshire figures is at a specialist dealer. A dealer will be knowledgable and will be able to answer most queries, but it should be remembered that he or she is running a business and it is therefore in their interests to sell you the figure. At a museum you will be able to see a broad range of figures, but not handle or buy them of course. Various auction rooms across the country will have view days where you can both see and handle the figures prior to a sale to assess their quality and value.

SPECIALIST DEALERS
A. & N. Harding
Tunbridge Wells
Antiques
12 Union Square
The Pantiles
Eridge Road
Royal Tunbridge Wells
Kent TN4 8HE, UK
Tel: 01892 533708
Nick@staffordshirefigures.com
Website:
www.staffordshirefigures.com

Jacquelin Oosthuizen
23 Cale Street
Chelsea Green
London SW3 3QR, UK
Tel: 020 7352 6071 or
020 7376 3852

Elinor Penna
P.O. Box 324
Old Westbury
New York 11568, USA
Tel: 001 800 294 0324/
001 516 294 4668

Ray Walker Antiques
Burton Arcade
296 Westbourne Grove
London W11 2PS, UK
Tel: 020 8464 7981
rwantiques@btinternet.com

ANTIQUES FAIRS
Antiques for Everyone
National Exhibition Centre
Birmingham B40 1NS, UK
(April, August & December)
Tel: 0121 767 4789

**British Antique Dealers'
Association Fair**
Duke of York's Headquarters
Cheltenham Terrace
London SW3, UK
(held annually in March)
Tel: 020 7589 6108

**The International Antique
& Collectors' Fair**
The Newark and Nottingham-
shire Showground, Newark,
Nottinghamshire NG24 2NY, UK
(held every other month)
Tel: 01636 720326

LAPADA Antiques Fair
Commonwealth Institute
Kensington High Street
London W8 6NQ, UK
(held annually in October)
Tel: 020 7767 4789

MAJOR AUCTION HOUSES
Bonhams Chelsea
65–9 Lots Road
London SW10 0RN, UK
Tel: 020 7393 3900
Website: www.bonhams.com

Bonhams Knightsbridge
Montpelier Street
London SW7 1HH, UK
Tel: 020 7393 3900

Butterfield & Butterfield
220 San Bruno Avenue
San Francisco CA 94103, USA
Tel: 001 415 861 7500

Christie's East
219 East 67th Street
New York NY 10021, USA
Tel: 001 212 606 0400
Website: www.christies.com

Christie's King Street
8 King Street
St James'
London SW1Y 6QT, UK
Tel: 020 7839 9060

Christie's New York
Rockefeller Centre
20 Rockefeller Plaza
New York NY 10020, USA
Tel: 001 212 636 2000

Christie's South Kensington
85 Old Brompton Road
London SW7 3LD, UK
Tel: 020 7581 7611

Phillips
101 New Bond Street
London W1Y 0AS, UK
Tel: 020 7629 6602
Website:
www.phillips-auctions.com

Phillips Bayswater
10 Salem Road
London W2 4DL, UK
Tel: 020 7229 9090

Phillips New York
Phillips, Son & Neale
406 East 79th Street
New York, NY 10021, USA
Tel: 001 212 570 4830

Skinner Inc.
357 Main Street
Bolton MA 01740, USA
Tel: 001 508 779 6241

Sotheby's
34–5 New Bond Street
London W1A 2AA, UK
Tel: 020 7293 5000
Website: www.sothebys.com

Sotheby's New York
1334 York Avenue
New York NY 10021, USA
Tel: 001 212 606 7000

MUSEUMS & COLLECTIONS
**The Potteries Museum
& Art Gallery**
Bethseda Street
Hanley
Stoke-on-Trent ST1 3DW, UK
Tel: 01782 232323

**Victoria and Albert
Museum**
Cromwell Road
South Kensington
London SW7 2RL, UK
Tel: 020 7942 2000

ASSOCIATIONS
**Art and Antique Dealers'
League of America (AADLA)**
353 East 78th Street
New York NY 10021, USA
Tel: 001 212 879 7558

**Association of Art and
Antiques Dealers (LAPADA)**
53 King's Road
London SW10 0SZ
Tel: 020 7351 4686

**British Antique Dealers'
Association (BADA)**
20 Rutland Gate
London SW7 1BD
Tel: 020 7589 4128

**National Art & Antiques
Dealers' Association
(NAADA)**
12 East 78th Street
New York NY 10021, USA
Tel: 001 212 826 9707

Index

Acknowledgments

Jacket photograph and picture p.2 by Steve Tanner © Octopus Publishing Group Ltd. All other pictures are the copyright of A. & N. Harding, Tunbridge Wells Antiques Centre. The publishers would also like to thank Jaqueline Oosthuizen for kindly supplying items for photography.